# A Circle of Love

# THE CHILDREN OF A CIRCLE OF LOVE

**2nd Grade Class,** Address Unknown (cover art); **Debosree,** Ewing, New Jersey (title page, pp. 9 & 28); **Julie,** Address Unknown (p. 10); **Jessica,** Wanaque, New Jersey (p. 11); **Charles,** University Park, Illinois (p. 12); **Margaret,** St. Louis, Missouri (p. 13); **Megan,** Ocean City, New Jersey (p. 14); **Name Unknown,** Ocean City, New Jersey (p. 15); **Vivian,** Skokie, Illinois (p. 16); **Ben,** Address Unknown (p. 17); **1st Grade Class,** Scarsdale, New York (p. 18); **Alycia,** Danvers, Minnesota (p. 19); **Phillip,** Arapaho, Oklahoma (p. 20); **Adam,** Aurora, Illinois (p. 21); **Mallory,** Fontana, California (p. 22); **Alix,** Buffalo Grove, Illinois (p. 23); **Katelyn,** Alberta, Canada (p. 24); **April,** South Boston, Massachusetts (p. 25); **Cathlene,** Michigan (p. 26); **Robert,** Waterbury, Connecticut (p. 27); **Kira,** Des Plaines, Illinois (p. 29); **Yelena,** Brooklyn, New York (p. 30); **Nick,** Saginaw, Michigan (pp. 30–31); **Lamont,** Chicago, Illinois (p. 31); **Adam,** Las Vegas, Nevada (p. 32); **Danielle,** Address Unknown (p. 33); **Melissa,** Address Unknown (p. 34); **Jackie,** West Chicago, Illinois (p. 34); **Julia,** Brookfield, Illinois (p. 35); **Pamela,** St. Petersburg, Florida (p. 36); **Nicole,** Saginaw, Michigan (pp. 37–40); **Dawn,** Address Unknown (p. 42); **Christopher,** Choctaw, Oklahoma (p. 43); **Erinn,** Lake Bluff, Illinois (p. 44); **Name Unknown,** Address Unknown (p. 45); **Maar,** Mount Prospect, Illinois (p. 46); **Sandra,** Bridgeport, Connecticut (p. 47); **Jed,** Denver, Colorado (p. 48); **Matt,** Skokie, Illinois 49); **Jonathan,** Kfar Saba, Israel (p. 50); **Emily,** Cerritos, California (p. 51); **Hannah,** Evanston, Illinois (p. 52); **Audra,** Ada, Oklahoma (p. 53); **Jacob,** Centerville, Tennessee (p. 54); **Eric,** Lawton, Oklahoma (p. 55); **Ashley,** Address Unknown (p. 56); **Kelsey,** Kingfisher, Oklahoma (p. 56); **Kathleen,** South Boston, Massachusetts (p. 57); **Clayton,** Del City, Oklahoma (p. 58); **Kenice,** East Northport, New York (p. 59); **Daniel,** Stillwater, Oklahoma (p. 60); **Ian,** Cumberland, Maryland (p. 61); **Stephanie,** Littleton, Colorado (paw prints, pp. 62–65); **Mark,** Ripley, Oklahoma (p. 62); **Andra,** Edmond, Oklahoma (p. 62); **Chad,** New Bedford, Massachusetts (p. 63); **Leslie,** Chicago, Illinois (p. 64); **Emily Anne,** Address Unknown (p. 65); **Amanda,** Address Unknown (p. 65); **Gina,** Address Unknown  (pp. 66–67); **Denise,** Del City, Oklahoma (p. 68); **Brandon,** Address Unknown (p. 69); **Kim,** Del City, Oklahoma (p. 70); **Mara,** Address Unknown (p. 71); **Mindy,** Bethany, Oklahoma (p. 72); **Name Unknown,** Oklahoma City, Oklahoma (p. 73); **Nathan,** Del City, Oklahoma (p. 74); **Jordan,** Oklahoma City, Oklahoma (p. 74); **Jeremy,** Oklahoma City, Oklahoma (p. 75); **Reuben,** Address Unknown (p. 76); **Eric,** Healdton, Oklahoma  (pp. 76–77); **Ryan,** Healdton, Oklahoma (p. 77); **Chris,** Oklahoma City, Oklahoma (p. 78); **Luke,** Woodstock, Georgia (p. 79); **Renee,** Alberta, Canada (p. 80).

*Frances Jones and the people of Oklahoma City would like to thank all the children who responded to us in our time of need.*

# A Circle of Love

## The Oklahoma City Bombing
## Through the Eyes of Our Children

COMPILED BY **FRANCES JONES**

EDITED BY **FRED CHASE**

Oklahoma City, Oklahoma

Library of Congress Catalog Card Number 96-94590
ISBN 0-9653320-0-4

Cover and Book Design by Songhee Kim
Production Assistant: Jeannie Rogers

Printed and bound in the United States of America by IPD Printing, Atlanta, Georgia

First Edition
10  9  8  7  6  5  4  3  2

Every effort has been made to contact the contributors whose letters and artwork are reproduced in this volume.

All proceeds received by Feed The Children from A CIRCLE OF LOVE will be used exclusively to aid children who are the victims of violence and/or disaster.

For information on how you or your family can be involved in the work of Feed The Children, please call or write to:

Feed The Children
P. O. Box 36
Oklahoma City, Oklahoma 73101
(405) 942-0228

Dedicated to the memory of the nineteen children who lost
their lives in the bombing of the Alfred P. Murrah Federal
Building, to the strength of the children who were affected
by the bombing, and to the spirit of all our children,
who show us each and every day that there is hope
for peace in the world.

# Introduction

*April 19, 1995, 9:02 A.M., Oklahoma City, Oklahoma*

Within a few days of the bombing of the Alfred P. Murrah Federal Building in Oklahoma City on April 19, 1995, letters began arriving at Feed The Children from the children of our nation to the children of Oklahoma City. In a period of two to three weeks, we received over 30,000 letters. Their simple, yet ofttimes mature, expressions of comfort and compassion allowed us to stay focused and functioning during the nightmare following the disaster.

While the letters were so helpful to me, they also filled a need from each young life to personally "do something" to help. Children in church groups, school classrooms, Boy Scouts, Girl Scouts, Brownies, athletic organizations, and Kids Clubs, in cities from California to Maine and from Florida to Canada, all wrote to offer encouragement to our hurting city. They poured out their hearts in sweetness and honesty in ways that only children can.

"Why?" is a question universal to us all. Why would someone do this? Why here? Why anywhere? Our nation's children tried to answer these questions through their insightful letters, each response individual unto itself. Some of the letters were simply printed in elementary scrawl while others were flawlessly typed in computer printout. Some were decorated with primary colors of crayon while others were designed with bold strokes of art. Regardless of size, color, shape, or content, all the letters spoke love to the victims and survivors of this senseless tragedy.

Children also sent letters of encouragement to firefighters and policemen, doctors and medical people, volunteer workers and ambulance drivers. Many of even the most seasoned disaster response teams would have been emotionally paralyzed if it had not been for the thank-yous from the children. And these brave men and women gave our children a new meaning to the word "hero."

To personally witness such terrible injuries and to hear rescue workers describe what they had seen was both overwhelming and depressing. However, as the children's letters poured in, I would often pick up a handful, take them to the solitude of my office . . . and read . . . and weep. And the tears that fell were always tears of release, washing away the despair I felt as I daily looked on the destruction that had wounded the innocence of childhood. During those moments when I thanked God for the freshness of young life revealed in the writing and artwork, I realized that these gifts from the heart begged to be shared with a grieving nation.

A CIRCLE OF LOVE offers a much needed message of hope. Our children have been frightened enough by the graphic descriptions and pictures that followed the bombing. Some children still have difficulty sleeping and separating from their parents if they go to a day school or preschool. Others fear their parents will not return home from work, or that they might be killed or injured. These concerns are not confined to children in Oklahoma. They are nationwide, indeed, worldwide.

I will never forget those tragic days of suffering . . . neither will I forget the tender responses of caring. Just as the children's letters healed my empty spaces and filled my empty places, my prayer is that they will soothe a shattered world and help renew our faith that God does, indeed, promise a brighter future, a future in which evil is overcome with good.

*Frances Jones*

# Here Are Some Kind Words for You

Dear Child,

I hope you're O.K. of what happened in Oklahoma.

And I hope your Family's okay too.

I can't come and comfort you, (in Oklahoma) but what I can do is pray for you. Here are some kind words for you, care, loving, sharing and happiness. Hope your okay!

Love, Julu

4th gr.
St. Leanord's S.

I drop you off to start the day
I drop you off you turn my way
You turn my way to say goodbye
This is the last time I would see you but I did not cry
I leave for work you start to have fun
little did I know your life was done
It will hurt my heart, it will hurt my soul
It will hurt my life I still dont want to let you go
I loved you so much now you'll know
What life had to give you you'd just begun to grow
I know god will hold you close and hold you near
Around him please don't fear
I can not sleep throw hours of pain
From this incident I have nothing to gain
You still have people who still love you much
All you have to do is hold out your hand and touch
Hold them close and don't let them go
Tell them you love them so they can know
I close with these words I won't skip one part
Take the love they gave you and put it in your heart.

Sorry, Oklahoma City

by Margaret

13

Dear Oklahoma City,
I'm sorry to
hear about what
happened. I'll tell
you a secret.
Sometimes I wish
I didn't have a
sister, but now
that I heard
this I'm glad
I have a sister.
Please write

Dear Oklahoma Child,

Don't be scared. I send my condolences to you and your family. Keep your hopes up! Just remember that I'm praying for you and I truly care. The people in your town are there to comfort you and the people nation-wide are also there to support you.

Are you going to be all right? In case you do get frightened, think about good things. Wonderful things, like: rainbows, lollipops, the season of summer, sunshine, giggles, birthday presents, raindrops on roses, whiskers on kittens, snowflakes, etc. Think of all the enjoyable things and memories that make you smile. (I will be very sad if you don't just smile a little bit.)

You know what? I think you are one of the bravest people in the whole entire nation! I would be hiding in a hole right now, like a rabbit. It's nice to see other people being so courageous and bold. I'm almost twelve and I'm scared of the littlest things. The other night at a school camping trip, we went on a night hike and I was really scared. The slightest movement made me jump! I guess I'm not as brave as you, huh? I'm not jealous of your hardy spirit, I'm really proud of you. (You may not think this of yourself, but I think you really are brave!)

Well, I better go now. But always remember to keep your hopes up and think the happiest thoughts! May the compassion of myself and others help guide you on your way.

Sincerely,
Vivian

# Hope Never Fails

Love Always
Will Remain
From, Ben

Dear freinds,

hope you feel better.

We raised money for you

and we made $175.

I feel bad for you.

We had bake-ins at our

homes. We made cupcakes,

brownies and cookies. We sold

that stuff. and made

that money. Kaeley,
            Love, Jenna, Casey,
        Gabriella, Monisha,
Jamie Laura, Jacob, Jonathan, Liza,
    Sarah, Dylan, Harrison,
Caitlin, Chiemi, Rachel, Reba.

18

19

Dear Everyone,

I'm sorry about the losses. Cry if you need to. Scream out your anger. I have lost two family members in the past five years. Again I am sorry. I understand. I know how it feels. I have been there. Again I am so so sorry.

Love to all with all my heart.
Phillip

P.S. I am from the Arapaho Fifth grade.

FAMILYS OF THE BOMBING

Dear families,

    We are all very sorry about what happend to your childern or family members. I would have been sad if my child was in that building. I hope you feel better after you read my letter. I am really sorry this terrible thing happened. Some people in the world are mean. I hope someday your broken heart will heal. I want you to know your family is in my prayers. I hope the man that did that bomb goes to jail for a long time. That man is mean for doing that bomb. I hope my letter will heal your pains.

                              SINCERELY,
                              MALLORY
                              Troop 11

23

Form Katelyn

May 3, 1995

Dear families
Hi. My name is
Katelyn. I am 6
years old.
I know
you are
sad.
I am very sorry
Sorry That it happened
I am a girl
and I saw it on t.v.
sincerely
Katelyn

I Loveyou People ... Iamxoxoxoxoxox
in . Iam sosad sad sosad
Oklahoma and from April.

I feel sad.

Dear Oklahoma City,

I know you're probably reading the same thing over and over, but I'd just like to let you know that all of the good people in Michigan are loving you and praying for you. I'm very sorry the bombing had to go on. I think it's terrible to have to wait for a tragedy to make our country closer.

I'm sorry I'm not sending much, but I'm only 13 years old and I don't have much spending money. I still have to pay for the shipping.

It feels like I knew the people who got killed or hurt because I all of a sudden break down as I am now.

I hope our country can help you with this. I'm praying for you. If you ever lose hope and need something positive to think about, think about me praying for you. Love and peace,
Cathlene

# WE ARE
# SORRY

*Oklahoma City

Oklahoma

# FROM

Connectict

* Waterbury

Dear Familie,
    When I hard
that your baby died I
was shoked!! Love.
    P.S. I'm sorry.    Débie

April, 26, 1995
10:05 A.M

Dear families of victims
in Oklahoma City,
    I feel really bad for you
and the people you know
that passed away. At 10:02,
A.M. we had a moment
of silence to think about
the terrorism that happened in
Oklahoma City. I know just how
you feel. My dad died
when I was five. This note I hope
makes you feel better. Write back
if you can. I will include
a picture of me and       Sincerely,
my dog.                        Yelena

Dear Friends,

I am sorry about your kids. Remember and cherish the times you had with them.

Always have hope don't give up.

Hi my name is Adam. I live in Las Vegas. I am writing to you because I hope and want you to get better. I think that the person who did this is very selfish. I bet he doesn't thank himself for doing it. Get Well.

I hope it look
like this
again

33

I
Love
YOU
KIDS
FROM

MELISSA

I AM
PRAYING
FOR YOU

God make
the people of
Oklahoma City
get well

# I understand
By: Pamela

I understand how the world turns grey,
When you think about that day.
How no one seems to see you there,
How no one ever seems to care.
How you feel deep in your heart,
How your life fits in a cart.
How tears fall down your face, so much,
How everyone needs a special touch.
How you need to cheer up,
Maybe you might find a pup.

How the world forgets you,
How you can't find anything new.

How you lose your best friend,
How you made letters to send.
How what you tried to prevent,
Is now a special current event.
How you have a feel to cry,
How you build up tears in your eyes.
When you come to us to care,
We will help, and we'll be there.

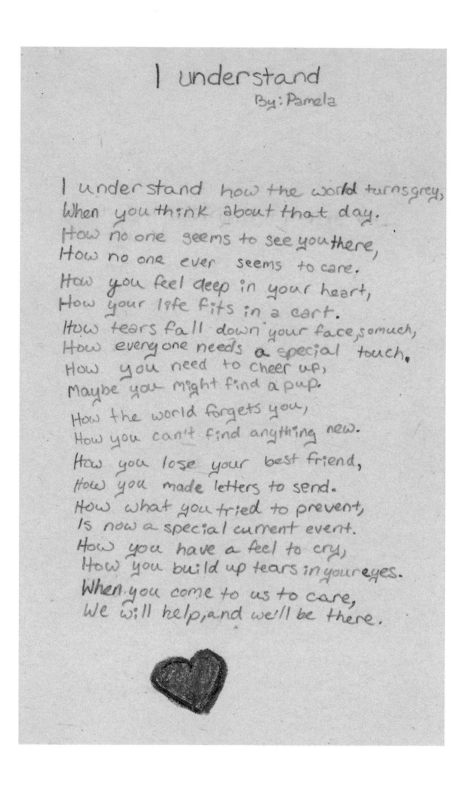

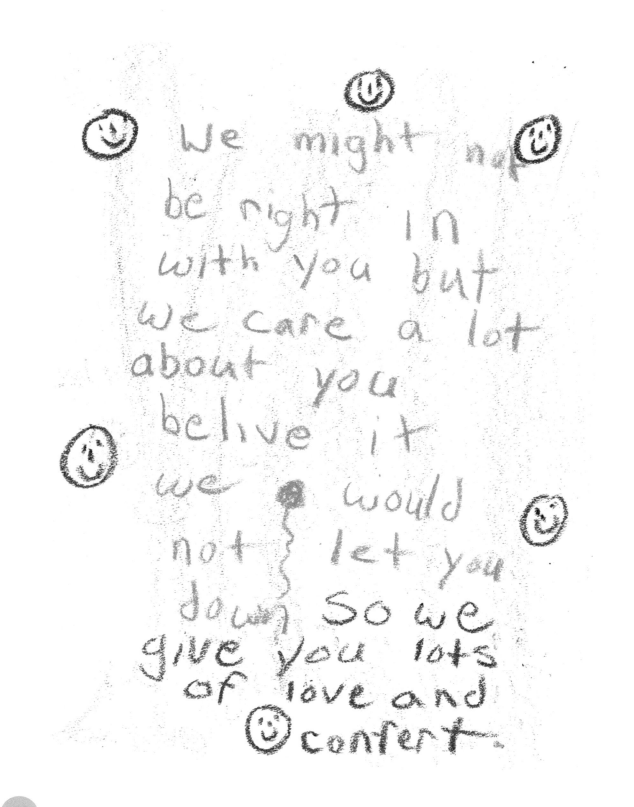

We might not
be right in
with you but
we care a lot
about you
belive it
we would
not let you
down so we
give you lots
of love and
comfort.

give happy smiles

let the
sun shine on
you                    over →

# Why

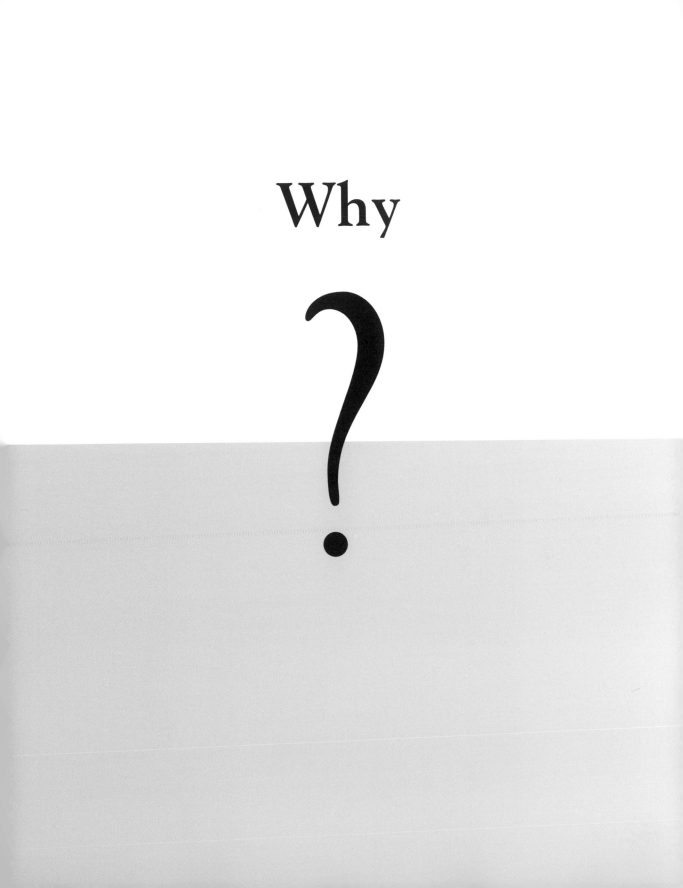

This is how I feel

about what happened

I AM
by: Christopher
age: 13


I am pained and confused
I wonder why many lives were taken because of someone else's hatred
I hear unknown children, needing someone to hold, cry in the presence of strangers trying
        to help
I see rain, God's tears showing His sympathy
I want someone to blame, to hate, but that's how this got started in the first place
I am pained and confused

I pretend we live in a world without hate or prejudice
I feel as if a piece of all of us has abruptly been taken
I touch my head as the dead touch my soul
I worry that the memory will not go away
I cry, "Why the innocent? Why children? Why death?"
I am pained and confused.

I understand the mourning from the ones whose loved one's whereabouts are unknown
I say I believe this, but doubt even myself
I dream this never happened
I try to face reality, but ignore the facts
I hope we are free of terrorism
I am pained and confused

Dear Friend,
 I am really sorry about what happened in Oklahoma City. You might not have been affected by it but you probably really hurt inside. All the kids that were killed meant a lot to people, and a lot to me. I mean, I might not have known them, they were kids, kids that did not get a life to live. It isn't fair.
 "How could someone do this!" I keep asking myself. How could someone do this to people who were innocent? Parents lost their kids, that's the worst thing that happend. And someone did do this.
 "Wow!" sorry, it's just I've never talked so serious before. I guess it's because I'm sad, really sad. It makes me mad, too. Mad at the people who did this.
 When I saw the picture of the man running out of the building carrying the baby that later died I cried. That man was brave and

so are the people who are still looking through the Federal Building and won't stop until they find everybody that was in there before the bomb went off. They are brave; Very, very brave. Please write back

Erinn       , age 10

# My Poem

We all know it was crime. It was all wrong at the wrong time. It was so big so fast it was the most biggest blast. We all have one question, for everyone everywhere why here, why there, why anywhere why Oklahoma such a sweet state what do we have to hate? The suspects some do some don't but they're is always hope.

May 8, 1995

Dear Friends,

I know I still don't understand anything and I'm sure you don't. Even though I wasn't there at that time, I understand your sadness. I'm not writing this letter because I have to, I want to. The recent bombing was terrible! It must be difficult. When I heard about the bombing I was terrified that the people who did this will do the same in every state. I wish there was something I could do. I'm sorry this happened.

Sincerely,
Maan

April 26, 1995

Its such a shame,
that a country so great,
could be so tragedy stricken
and full of hate.
There's so much corruption,
that nothing seems quite right.
Then the innocent people,
are the ones to pay the price.
I can almost understand,
and I'm almost quite sure,
that there's no longer a reason,
to really feel secure.
Everything is lost,
and the pain is too great.
Now I think I know,
the price of such hate.
Like I said before,
It's a shame, what a pity.
I really feel for those,
in Oklahoma City.

Sandra
    Grade 8
    P.C.M.N.C.

April 27, 1995

Dear People of Oklahoma:

It is very hard for me to say how I feel about this incident that occured earlier this month. A million feelings come to mind when I think about the bombing. Sadness, anger, grief, and hate all run through me when I see the awful destruction done & and the precious lives lost. I cannot even imagine how the children who survived, or even the adults who survived, can understand why this happened to them. The whole country grieves for the deaths of innocent people. I hope with all of my heart your state will recover and the people put to justice who committed this awful crime.

Sincerely yours,

Jed                                    7th Grade

In memory and honor of all the men, women, and children killed and injured in the bombing.

I think that this bombing is a disgrace. A disgrace not only to the United States, but to me, the entire world, and to put it plainly, to mankind. To think that someone could be so thoughtless, just because of anger. Anger can be overcome, can be made as if to never have existed. Death, on the other hand, cannot. To even *think* about taking the lives of innocent, *innocent*, men, women, and children, to even *think* about taking the lives of innocent sons, daughters, fathers, mothers, cousins, aunts, uncles, friends and loved ones, to even *think* about taking all from people for which they have to live for, is inhumane. It is unthinkable. This was not an attack on the United States, but an attack on life, and all of its basic principals.

The explosion was sad because lots of innocent people were killed.
Horrible people make explosions and they should go to jail
Even little day care children were killed


Everybody remembers the bomb
Xrays are needed for the wounded
President Clinton is going to give a reward to the people who find the people who planted the bomb
Lots of people were found dead and more and more are being found
Oklahoma is where the bomb was
Stupid people plant bombs.
Instead of making peace
Only G-d knows why it happened if any body knows
Nobody, I hope, will ever plant a bomb that will kill so many people again

Jonathan          3A

Dear Oklahoma City,

I am a fourth grader at Mary Bragg. I was terrified when I saw on TV that the federal building had been bombed. I just couldn't bear the sight of it.

Even if I'm a fourth grader, I feel sorry for the people who were hurt and those who died. Our fourth grade recently did a peace program and I don't think this fits very well with it.

I hope you will feel better. I am very ashamed of the people who bombed the building.

Sincerely,
Emily

# A Bombing

Hannah

A nation in tears.

Bells clang, similar to a funeral.

A nation of fears.

People realize that this could happen to anyone.

People begin to cry.

A nation of tears.

They see pictures of children who are dead.

Why do these babies have to die?

All because of a few ignorant people.

People despair.

A nation losing hope.

We want the criminals brought to justice.

Isn't there any way we can prepare?

Can't we stop this useless bloodshed?

A nation despairs.

Why?

Who could do this to innocent children?

Why do people have to die?

Why this outrageous act of violence?

What are we doing to help?

A nation struggles with questions.

America is supposed to be without fear.

It is supposed to be free of terrorists.

These images flow away with each tear.


A nation wonders.

These useless slaughters occur in other places, I know.

But it really hurts when the tragedy strikes close to home.

## Sadness So Sudden

When I ly in my bed I
Wonder what God intends
For me to do tomorrow
I lay and suddenly a tear
Rolls down my cheak, I
Start to think and ponder
Why all the chidren and
Parent all died. I start
To ask God why he let
Them die so sudden, but
Then I stopped myself.
I said to myself God
Didn't do it two people
On God's green earth
Did the sudden bomb.
Then I drifted off to
sleep.

I'm sorry.

name          age
Jacob          7      boy✗ girl✗

54

# I Know Now There Is Good In The World

Dear fireman

I see you on Tv and you lock very tird and you are dowing a good Job helping to get the people out. and I said a prayer for you to day at church this morning. Ashley 8

Because of you she'll live

*Clayton*

To the Rescue workers,

     If this had happened a day earlier I would be writing a different letter. My mother works several blocks away and had gone to the credit union the previous afternoon. She knows several of the adults and children that were injured and killed. With all the stress that you are under let this thought comfort you. Every person you save has friends and family that love them. You aren't just saving one person you're fulfilling hope for dozens of people. Thanks.

*Clayton*

from: Kenice

you may not be
a hero to yourself
but you are to us

you have
saved so many
Lives.
Thank you

Thank You for saving
people.

by Daniel

thank you

Thank you for giving your life for people.
you are the Real Heros!

Your Friend,
Ian

Cumberland MD

Dear, Rescue Dogs

You are working hard at
finding People it must
be scare in that bulding

I like animals alot

RESCUE
DOG

Your'er
friend
mark

Dear Policeman

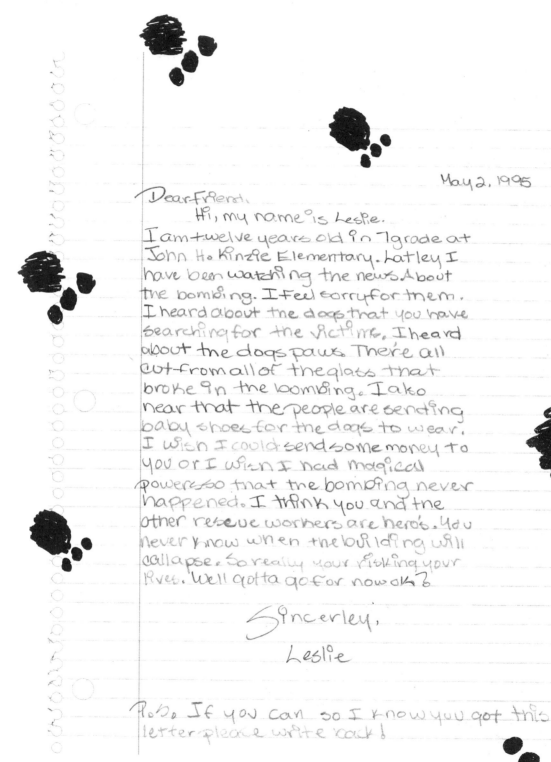

May 2, 1995

Dear Friend,

Hi, my name is Leslie.
I am twelve years old in 7 grade at
John H. Kinzie Elementary. Latley I
have been watching the news About
the bombing. I feel sorry for them.
I heard about the dogs that you have
searching for the victims. I heard
about the dogs paws. There all
cut from all of the glass that
broke in the bombing. I also
heard that the people are sending
baby shoes for the dogs to wear.
I wish I could send some money to
you or I wish I had magical
powers so that the bombing never
happened. I think you and the
other rescue workers are hero's. You
never know when the building will
collapse. So really your risking your
lives. Well gotta go for now ok?

Sincerley,

Leslie

P.S. If you can so I know you got this
letter please write back!

64

Dear Rescue Dogs,

you've been great you diserve 1,000,000 doggie treats. thanks alot.

Sincenly,
Emily
Anne

Dear Puppy Dogs,

Don't quit, Don't get depressed. Ceep on going when an opsticle appears. Jump on over and come on down. My heart is with you.

Love,
Amanda

Thanks for making Mom
nice and importend
to help but I'm
and have to go to
was cring because I
I feel so sorry

happy you are so
to me I would like
nd an Aldult like you
school my mom
bies died in the bon
for the babies that died

Gina          Second Gradr

DEAR RESCUE WORKER,

I am writing to show my appreciation and gratitude for your tiersome efforts. Your bravery made me as well as others proud and your compasion made us sympathitic to your cause. Tears of pain ran down my face as I saw the devistation. The destruction of lives and the scaring of souls made my heart hurt. But when I saw you on television working so diligently, you inspired me, giving me hope and a renewel of strength. My thougtits are with you. I wanted to express my love for you through this letter. I know I won't be able to take away the pain, but I wanted you to know your work wasn't in vain. You helped bring a nation together; a nation that looked past color, religion, and other diffrences to see the similarities between one another. What we discovered was a bond so strong that not even this disaster could tear us apart. This is what makes you great; this is what makes you a hero.

Love,

Denise

Dear Volunteers,

I would like to thank you for your bravery and courage.

I could never tell you in words how much what you are doing means to Oklahoma. I can't imagen what you have seen but know that it will be worth it in the end. Seeing everyone helping on t.v. and hearing all the stories of support I know now there is good in the world. Thank you,

Kim
Del City H.S.

April 24, 1995

Dear Rescue Workers,

We as all the Americans would like to thank you for all your hard work. It means alot to all of us that you will give your time and help to look for survivors and the dead of the bombing.

What one or two mens hateful heart can ruin the lives of many. But thanks to your help it is lifting the spirits of many people around the world.

Reality is now starting to settle in that we as the children and young adults are not safe from the evil of this world.

And my six year old sister said the day it was raining "God is crying for the dead."

We thank you for your wonderful help.

God bless you all,
Mindy
Bethany Middle School

"Do unto others as you would want them to do to you."
<u>[you have done this]</u>

Dear sir's,

I would like to thank you for all your courageous help that you have given in our time of need. All of you there have inspired us to pull together as a state and be, not individuals in this crisis, but a state wide family. Your courage has inspired hundreds of people to help. In some way, all of us has been affected by this tragedy. Some more that others, but this tragedy has touched all of our life.

The way the entire state has pulled together the way we have, makes me proud to be an Okie for the first time in my life. I have always wanted to live somewhere more exciting until this disaster. Then I realized, that Oklahoma is a laid back, kind of state. It is a good place to come to raise a family, and feel secure about your children.

It's hard to imagine that someone would be so sadistic, to destroy a building with so many people in it, including the children. All those children that were in that building will never have the chance to do some of the simple things in life, like ride a bike, go to school, fall in love, or have a family of their own. That manic who did this robbed us of something special. They robbed us of some of our children, because all of the people in that building was someones child.

My heart goes out to you, and all of you helping.

God bless you all,
Nathan
Del City High School

To,
The firefighters.

I hope you feel good because I don't. I hope there is more saviors. I hope you go home and hug your kids

your freind

Jeremy

75

April 26th 95

Dear Volunteers,

Although I don't live in Oklahoma or even in your country I would like to thank you for your endless effort in finding the victims of the bombing. Hopefully the criminals in this bombing will be brought to justice and your efforts will be recongized.

Even though April 19th will be remembered for the victims and the criminals. I will remember the efforts of the volunteers as well, Thank you

Sincerely,
Reuben

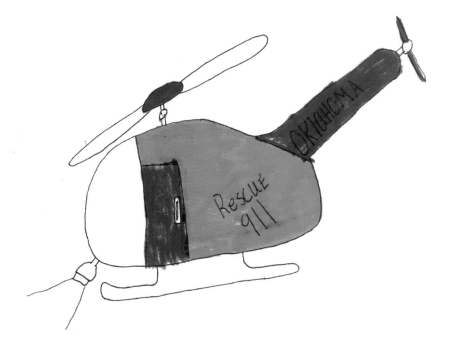

Dear Rescue Workers,

We are very sorry
for what has happened.
I hope you are careful
in that building. Even
if you don't pull out any
more survivers I will still
love you.

Eric
4th grade
Healdton Elem.
Carter County, OK

Peace

Peace to the world,
Peace to all;
Peace to the Children,
Peace in the fall;
Peace in the springtime,
In the Winter too,
Peace, Peace, what to do,
Peace, Peace, for me and you.

Chris            , Age 10

This poem was composed for the victims and rescuers of this tragedy.